4 How do fish get their teeth cleaned?

5 How can you tell a crocodile from an alligator?

6 Based on the shape of the teeth, was this dinosaur a meat eater or plant eater?

YOU CAN FIND THE ANSWERS TO THESE TOOTHY TIDBITS AT THE BACK OF THE BOOK.

OPEN WIDE!

THE ULTIMATE GUIDE TO TEETH

THE ULTIMATE GUIDE TEETH

Susan Grigsby

SEA GRASS

Quarto is the authority on a wide range of topics.
Quarto educates, entertains, and enriches the lives of our readers—
enthusiasts and lovers of hands-on living.
www.quartoknows.com

Produced by Scout Books & Media Inc
President and Project Director Susan Knopf
Editorial Team Brittany Gialanella, Michael Centore, Chelsea Burris
Index Andrea Baron
Page Layout DKD&AD

6 Orchard Road, Suite 100, Lake Forest, CA 92630
quartoknows.com
Visit our blogs at quartoknows.com

Printed in China
1 3 5 7 9 10 8 6 4 2

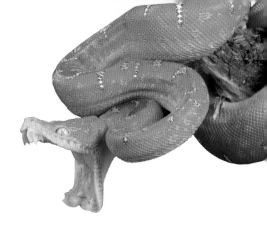

TABLE OF CONTENTS

THE WIDE WORLD OF TEETH

People are special in many ways. We have amazing minds that we can use for inventing and experimenting and finding the best ways to take care of others. But there also ways in which we're not so different from animals on this planet. Our mouths, teeth, and health have a lot in common with many other creatures, from extinct dinosaurs to family pets like dogs and cats.

WHAT IS A TOOTH?

A tooth is a hard structure in the mouth of a vertebrate (an animal with a backbone). Mammals (including people) are vertebrates. So are reptiles, amphibians, fish, and birds. Dinosaurs were vertebrates, too. Some vertebrates have teeth and some don't. The differences between teeth can be as amazing as the similarities.

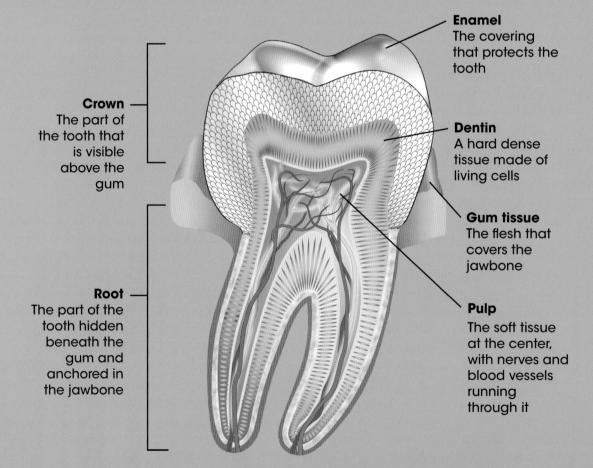

Enamel
The covering that protects the tooth

Crown
The part of the tooth that is visible above the gum

Dentin
A hard dense tissue made of living cells

Gum tissue
The flesh that covers the jawbone

Root
The part of the tooth hidden beneath the gum and anchored in the jawbone

Pulp
The soft tissue at the center, with nerves and blood vessels running through it

MAMMALS: SPECIAL TEETH FOR SPECIAL JOBS

Mammals are animals fed milk by their mothers. Almost all mammals have teeth. Unlike other vertebrates, most mammals with teeth have more than one shape of tooth in their mouths. This means they can chew food into smaller pieces. As adults, people have four basic tooth shapes, and each shape has a special job to do.

Incisor

Incisors are at the front of the mouth. They are sharp and straight across at the top. They can bite into food and then cut, chop, or gnaw it.

Canine

Canines are on both sides of the incisors. They are pointed and can pierce or stab food and tear it into smaller pieces

Premolar

Molar

Premolars and Molars can chew, crush, and grind up food into pieces small enough to be swallowed and digested. Premolars are between the canines and the molars. They are wide and have ridges on the surface. Molars are at the back of the mouth.

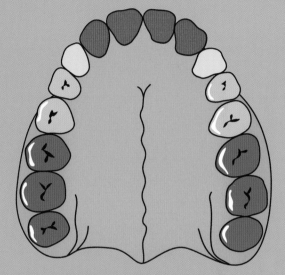

WHO ELSE HAS TEETH?

Nutria are large rodents that use strong front teeth to gnaw through plants, roots, and tree bark.

ORANGE CHOMPERS

Beavers, nutria, and many other rodents are different from most other mammals because they have iron in the enamel on the front side of their incisors. The iron, which colors the teeth orange, provides extra strength for gnawing. The iron also prevents decay.

A rodent's front incisor teeth are called ever growing because they are rootless and will grow throughout its life. The teeth continually wear away as they chew on hard, tough foods.

THE POWER OF ENAMEL

Our teeth, and the teeth of almost all other toothed vertebrates, are covered in enamel. Tooth enamel is the strongest substance in our bodies. It protects our teeth—which is important, because we need our teeth to survive. The next hardest substances in our bodies are bones and dentin, which is just below the enamel on our teeth.

MEET THE GULPERS

Some reptiles, fish, and amphibians have teeth. They are usually all cone shaped with a sharp point to pierce, stab and tear. It's not possible to chew food with pointed teeth, so these animals gulp their food.

Amphibians Many frogs have tiny sharp teeth to hold onto their prey before they swallow it whole. Toads do not have teeth.

Reptiles Alligators use their teeth to capture and hold prey while they drown it. Snakes with fangs, like rattlesnakes, use them to inject venom into prey.

Fish Piranhas have razor-sharp teeth and a powerful bite. Their name means "tooth fish."

INVERTEBRATES CLOSE-UP: INSECTS

Mosquitoes don't have teeth, but they can bite. They do this by piercing the skin with needlelike mouthparts that work like a straw to suck up blood.

Beetles have powerful jaws called mandibles that are hard and toothlike. Mandibles can be used to bite, chew food, capture prey, or fight.

Tooth Clues For Scientists

Teeth provide clues to scientists in fields from A to Z. Anthropologists study human cultures. They might look at this weapon made from sharks' teeth to learn about the people who made it. Zoologists study animal life. They might look at the teeth on the weapon to learn which sharks lived near the people who made it. Each species of shark has its own unique teeth.

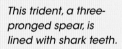

This trident, a three-pronged spear, is lined with shark teeth.

TOOTH TRUTH

Some animals, like birds and turtles, don't have teeth. But they do have an egg tooth, which is a hard, toothlike bump on the beak. The egg tooth is used to break out of the shell. It falls off soon after the animal hatches.

This red-eared slider still has its egg tooth.

TOOLS FOR SURVIVAL

Animals have teeth that help them catch and eat the food they need to survive and thrive.

Bengal tigers are CARNIVORES. This means they eat meat. They hunt large prey like deer, wild cattle, and boar. They use their large, sharp incisors and canines to grab and kill prey and rip flesh from the bones. Their molars have sharp points and ridges to slice food into smaller pieces.

HERBIVORES are animals that eat plants. They use incisors to chop off bite-size pieces of plants. Their molars are flat and wide for grinding and chopping plant parts. If they have canines, they are usually small. Some, like hippos, use them for fighting and self-defense.

Most humans are OMNIVORES. Omnivores are animals that regularly eat both plants and animals. With four different kinds of teeth, people can chew and grind up all kinds of food. The sun bear, an omnivore from Southeast Asia, eats fruit, honey, insects, and small animals such as birds and rodents.

WHAT MAKES A TUSK A TUSK?

African elephants have two impressive incisor teeth—their tusks. They are permanent incisors, on the top, that continue to grow throughout their lives. Both males and females have tusks, and they use them to dig for water and food, to pull bark off of trees, to lift or push heavy objects, and to defend their territory. African elephant tusks can grow to over 10 feet long and weigh up to 100 pounds each.

In addition to elephants, walruses, narwhals, and hippos all have ivory tusks.

THE LARGEST TEETH IN THE WORLD

African elephants have four molars, and each one weighs about five pounds. These large herbivores chew about 300 pounds of plants and tree bark a day. This wears down their molars. Luckily, they get six sets of molars in their lifetime. As teeth wear down, they slowly move forward and are replaced in the rear. The worn-down teeth eventually fall out.

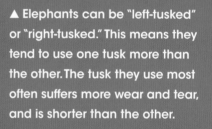

▲ Elephants can be "left-tusked" or "right-tusked." This means they tend to use one tusk more than the other. The tusk they use most often suffers more wear and tear, and is shorter than the other.

Narwhals have two teeth, but only one grows into a swordlike tusk. It grows through the upper lip and spirals outward, growing to 9 feet on males. Some females also grow tusks, but smaller ones. Narwhals are often called "unicorns of the sea."

TOOTHY
ADAPTATIONS

Animals have special body parts and behaviors adapted to where they live. Teeth play a big part in all sorts of environments, from cold to hot, wet to dry, and high to low.

JAWS WIDE OPEN

Eating on land provides carnivores time to devour their entire prey. Eating in water is trickier. The great white shark can push its jaws forward to grab prey with its sharp teeth. It then pulls its jaws—and the prey—back into its mouth. The pointed lower teeth hold on while the jagged uppers slice into the prey.

ICE PICKS

Walruses are also called tooth walkers, and they do use their tusks to drag their big bodies around on the slippery ice of their Arctic habitat. Between meals, they rest on ice floes. Lifting 2,000 pounds out of the water is a tough trick. Walruses do it by hooking their tusks into the ice. They also use their tusks to get to their underwater food supply, such as clams and shellfish. When the water surface freezes, they chip out a hole with their mighty tusks.

GOOD BATS

Flying foxes, also called fruit bats, live in warm areas where fruit grows year-round. They eat fruit, nectar, pollen, and flowers. They have special teeth to pierce through a fruit's outer skin or rind. Then they lap up the fruit through the cut they made. These bats are good for the environment, spreading seeds and pollinating plants.

WHEN THE ANTS COME MARCHING BY

The hot dry desert of Australia is home to the thorny devil. This small lizard eats only ants. When it finds a trail of ants, it waits for them to pass by. Then it uses its sticky tongue to flick them into its mouth. Its teeth are perfectly adapted to chewing thousands of crunchy ants per meal.

DIG THIS

Meet an animal with a confusing name. Mole rats are not moles or rats, but they are rodents. And naked mole-rats aren't totally naked. They have about 100 tiny whiskerlike hairs on their bodies. They live underground, where they use their sharp teeth to dig a network of tunnels. They eat tough roots and other underground plants. Their lower incisor teeth can move independently from each other. This special ability lets them move and carry objects in a motion similar to a pair of chopsticks that open and close.

11

PET TEETH FACTS AND OTHER ANIMALS

DO use a brush made especially for pets. It should have soft bristles and be small enough to fit into its mouth. Use special pet toothpaste. (Toothpaste made for people can make animals very ill.)

DO have a veterinarian show your family step-by-step how to get your pet used to home brushings.

Pets got to vets (veterinarians) for regular check-ups. The visit may include a professional tooth cleaning. Pets also need their teeth cleaned at home. There are special finger brushes, or long-handled brushes that keep your hands away from nipping teeth.

TOOTH TRUTH

Most mammals, including people, get two sets of teeth. The first set is called primary or baby teeth. The second set is called permanent teeth. Rodents get two sets of teeth, but they loose their baby teeth before they are even born. Dolphins get only one set, and keep their baby teeth their entire life.

Some pets have no teeth. These include chickens and turtles.

THE CASE OF THE MISSING TOOTH

Puppies and kittens have more primary teeth than people do. So where do all of the lost teeth go? Many are swallowed when they're eating, but if you are walking barefoot through the house, you might feel your pet's lost tooth before you see it. If you find one, you could place it under their pillow for a visit from a tooth fairy. What gift would your pet receive in return?

HOW MANY TEETH GET LOST?

BUNNY — 16 PRIMARY TEETH

BABY — 20 PRIMARY TEETH

COLT — 24 PRIMARY TEETH

PUPPY — 28 PRIMARY TEETH

SHARK — 30,000–50,000 OVER ITS LIFETIME

HAVE A BITE

• Rabbits eat plants. They are born with erupted (visible) primary teeth.

• Leopard geckos are born with 100 teeth. They grow new teeth to replace the old ones every three to four months.

▼ Hamsters' bottom teeth are longer than their top teeth.

CLUES TO THE PAST

Tyrannosaurus rex

Fossils are the preserved remains or traces of animals, plants, and other living things.

The shape of a fossilized tooth can provide clues to what animal it belonged to, how it was used, what the animal ate, and what its environment was like.

Most dinosaurs had only one tooth shape in their entire mouth. That shape was not the same for all dinosaurs. The shape matched with the work the dinosaur needed to do to get its food. Paleontologists group the dinosaur tooth shapes by describing the job they did. Do any of these seem similar to the different teeth in your mouth?

Rippers A meat-eating dinosaur like this Tyrannosaurus rex had a whole mouth full of knifelike teeth to stab their prey. The teeth were slightly curved to hook into the flesh, tear it from the bones, and gulp it down whole.

Choppers A plant-eater like the Triceratops used its toothless beak to snip off leaves. It had up to 800 sharp, chisellike teeth, arranged in rows, to chop up tough plants before swallowing them.

Grinders Edmontosaurus, a duck-billed dinosaur, had rows of tiny, flat-topped teeth for grinding up plants.

Strippers Long, blunt, peg-shaped teeth allowed long-necked dinosaurs to grasp onto lots of branches at one time, then strip off the leaves or bark and swallow it. A Titanosaur weighed about 70 tons (140,000 pounds)—it had to rake in a lot of food to survive.

KNOW A PRO: PALEONTOLOGIST

Paleontologists study all extinct creatures, not just dinosaurs. This fossil is from a mammal that lived about 10,000 years ago.

The 20,000-pound Columbian mammoth used its long tusks to forage for plants to eat.

HOW DO WE KNOW ABOUT DINOSAUR TEETH?

Teeth and bones are made of minerals, so they were most likely to become fossils when dinosaurs died.

Eryops

PALEOZOIC ERA
545–252 Million Years Ago
Fish, sharks, reptiles, amphibians, and land plants appeared.

Triassic Period
252–200 Million Years Ago
The first dinosaurs appeared. They were mostly small carnivores. Mammals appeared too.

Herrerasaurus

Stegosaurus

Cretaceous Period
145–66 Million Years Ago
Dinosaurs continued to thrive. Then, 66 million years ago, they became extinct.

Tyrannosaurus rex

Jurassic Period
200–145 Million Years Ago
Big dinosaurs thrived. Flowering plants appeared toward the end of this period. They became food for herbivores.

MESOZOIC ERA 252–66 Million Years Ago
Dinosaurs appeared. This era is known as the Age of Dinosaurs.

Woolly mammoth and baby

Saber-toothed tiger

CENOZOIC ERA
66 Million Years Ago—Present Day
Large mammals appeared, including mammoths and saber-toothed tigers. By about 200,000 years ago, the first modern humans (*homo sapiens*) appeared. We are still in the Cenozoic Era.

15

HELLO, TEETH!

At Birth

By the time a baby is born, the primary teeth have almost finished forming. There are ten on the top and ten on the bottom, but you can't see them. They are growing in the jawbone, which is covered by the gums.

At 6 to 12 Months

Teething begins as the primary teeth start to erupt, pushing through the gum.

By 33 to 36 Months

All 20 primary teeth have appeared.

Between 6 and 14 Years of Age

Baby teeth begin to fall out, one at a time. Permanent teeth grow in their place. They are larger and there are more of them—28! They all fit because the jawbone has grown.

Between 17 and 21 Years of Age

Four more teeth, called third molars or wisdom teeth, bring the total tooth count to 32. For one in three people, the wisdom teeth never grow in.

Sound It Out

Teeth help us speak clearly. There are some sounds that simply can't be made without them. Here's a look at how we make different sounds.

1 Babies don't have teeth, so they make sounds by putting their lips together. Try these:
ma-ma-ma
pa-pa-pa
ba-ba-ba
Did you need your teeth to make these sounds? These are called BILABIAL sounds (*bi* means "two" and *labia* means "lip"). So now you know why the first word a baby says is usually *ma* or *mom*.

2 Sounds made with some letters, such as F and V, are made by touching the upper teeth to the bottom lip. These are called LABIODENTAL sounds (using lips and teeth).
Five very fancy fish floated on a raft of velvet flowers.

3 Sounds such as *the* and *this* are made by placing the tongue between the upper and lower front teeth. The tongue touches the upper teeth to make these sounds, called INTERDENTAL (*inter* means "between").
Ruth thinks that the thunder is an ogre's thumb thumping on a leather drum.

maman 🇫🇷 France

MËMË Albania

mamma 🇮🇹 Italy

mati Croatia

maji India

Most words in the world for *mother* have the *M* sound in them.

madre 🇲🇽 Mexico

mom 🇺🇸 United States

mama Poland

Mutter Germany

ANIMALS OUR TEETH DEPEND ON

The milk we need for healthy teeth and bones comes from animals in a group called ruminants. Dairy cows, water buffalo, goats, and sheep are all ruminants. Only the females make milk.

Most ruminants are toothless across the front upper jaw. In place of upper incisors and canines, they have a thick dental pad.

- First pass
- Chewing the cud
- Moving through the digestive system
- Nutrients are absorbed; waste leaves the body

CHEWING CUD

Cows and other ruminants have to work hard to get enough nutrients from the plants and grasses they eat. Their stomachs have four different areas called chambers.

- First, they chew and swallow their food. It travels to an area called the rumen.
- The food is broken down and softens.
- Then it is regurgitated (returns to the mouth) as cud. It is chewed again.
- Finally, the food moves through the digestive system.

WHICH ANIMALS PROVIDE MILK FOR PEOPLE TO DRINK?

Animal	Percentage
CATTLE	83%
BUFFALO	13%
GOATS	2%
SHEEP	1%
CAMELS	0.4%
YAKS AND OTHER ANIMALS	0.6%

Camels use their upper incisors and canines to eat tough plants in the desert habitat where they live.

Milk Menu

For more than 6 billion people in the world, milk products are a part of their diet. Which of these milk-based foods would you like to eat?

Swiss Cheese (Switzerland)

MILK

Mac and Cheese (United States)

Gelato (Italy)

Flan (Brazil)

Goat Cheese (France)

Yogurt (Greece)

Black Forest Cake (Germany)

Bubble Tea (Taiwan)

PRIMARY AND PERMANENT TEETH

BABY TEETH

Our baby teeth are called primary because they are our first set. When a person is born, the crowns (tops) of their primary teeth are already under the gums, but they don't have roots. As the root of a tooth grows, its crown is forced through the gums. This takes place one tooth at a time, until all 20 baby teeth have come in.

Each baby tooth holds a space in the proper place for a permanent tooth. Its root helps guide the permanent tooth growing below it to the right spot. When a permanent tooth starts to grow in the jaw, it presses on the baby tooth root above it. This slowly breaks down the root of the baby tooth until it's nearly dissolved. Then the tooth loosens. After a baby tooth is shed, the permanent tooth doesn't come in right away. It is still growing and will eventually push its way into place.

JUST LIKE US
Chimpanzees have the same number of baby and adult teeth, and the same tooth types and tooth arrangement as people do. Their canine teeth are larger and sharper than ours.

WHEN DO BABY TEETH COME AND GO?

Most Primary Teeth Erupt and Shed in This Order:	HOW MANY WE GET	AGE WHEN THEY ERUPT	AGE WHEN THEY SHED
CENTRAL INCISOR	🦷🦷🦷🦷	6–12 MONTHS	6–7 YEARS
LATERAL (SIDE) INCISOR	🦷🦷🦷🦷	9–16 MONTHS	7–8 YEARS
FIRST MOLAR	🦷🦷🦷🦷	13–19 MONTHS	9–11 YEARS
CANINE	🦷🦷🦷🦷	16–23 MONTHS	9–12 YEARS
SECOND MOLAR	🦷🦷🦷🦷	23–36 MONTHS	10–12 YEARS

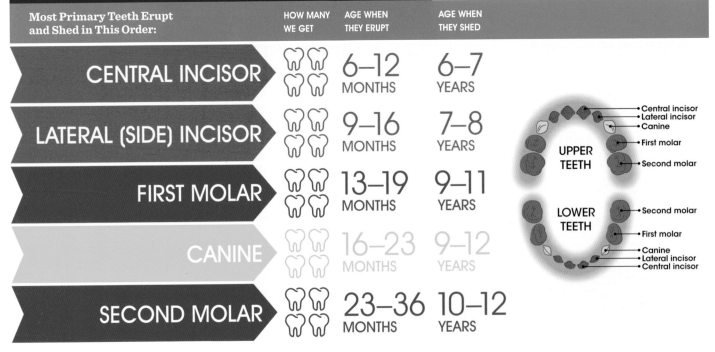

UPPER TEETH
- Central incisor
- Lateral incisor
- Canine
- First molar
- Second molar

LOWER TEETH
- Second molar
- First molar
- Canine
- Lateral incisor
- Central incisor

PERMANENT TEETH

Permanent incisors and canines erupt in the same place that the baby incisors were. Permanent premolars erupt where the primary first and second molars were. Since the permanent teeth are bigger, how do they fit? You are growing at the same time! Your jawbone gets longer at the back, which makes space for the permanent molars. The permanent first, second, and third molars form in new jaw growth at the back.

WHEN DO PERMANENT TEETH GROW IN?

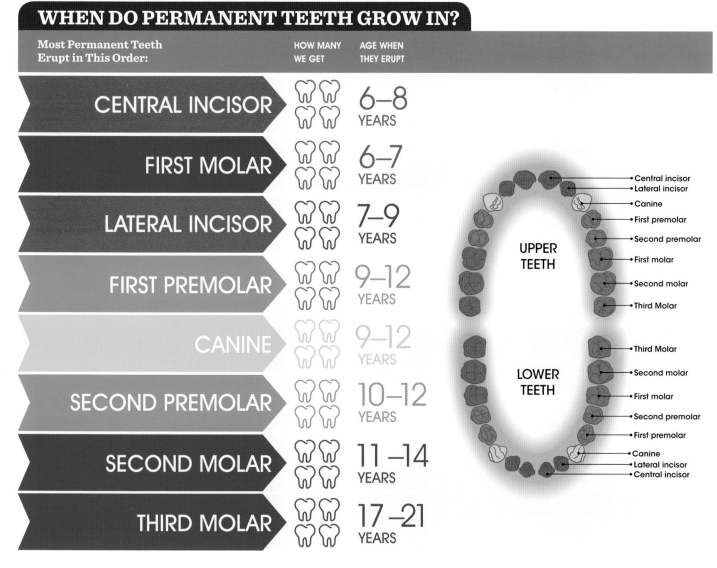

Most Permanent Teeth Erupt in This Order:	HOW MANY WE GET	AGE WHEN THEY ERUPT
CENTRAL INCISOR		6–8 YEARS
FIRST MOLAR		6–7 YEARS
LATERAL INCISOR		7–9 YEARS
FIRST PREMOLAR		9–12 YEARS
CANINE		9–12 YEARS
SECOND PREMOLAR		10–12 YEARS
SECOND MOLAR		11–14 YEARS
THIRD MOLAR		17–21 YEARS

UPPER TEETH

LOWER TEETH

- Central incisor
- Lateral incisor
- Canine
- First premolar
- Second premolar
- First molar
- Second molar
- Third Molar
- Third Molar
- Second molar
- First molar
- Second premolar
- First premolar
- Canine
- Lateral incisor
- Central incisor

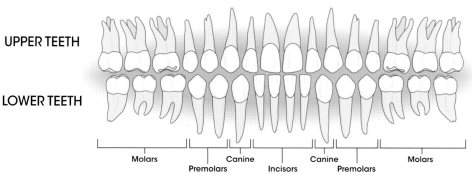

UPPER TEETH

LOWER TEETH

Molars | Premolars | Canine | Incisors | Canine | Premolars | Molars

Root Counts

Incisor and canine teeth each have just one root. A premolar can have one or two roots. A molar tooth can have two or three roots.

GOODBYE, TOOTH!

Losing a baby tooth is an important part of growing up. People mark this special occasion in many different ways. Here are just a few traditions from around the globe.

Make a Wish When You Lose a Tooth

• Do you want a small gift, sweet, or money? Hide the tooth and make your wish to a tooth fairy, magical mouse, or leprechaun.

• To wish for the new tooth to be strong, toss it to a squirrel, rabbit, rat, or mouse. They have strong incisor teeth that grow continually. That's why we involve them when we wish for strong teeth.

• Do you want a bright and healthy new tooth? Then throw it up toward the sun.

ROAR

The baby teeth on this lion cub look sharp, but they're tiny compared to the adult teeth that will grow in.

KEEPING MEMORIES
Some people save their baby teeth in a special place. A small treasure box holds just one tooth, and a larger one will hold all your lost baby teeth.

NATIONAL TOOTH FAIRY DAY
FEBRUARY 28

The Little Tooth Mouse trades coins for teeth in countries all over the world. In one tradition, a baby tooth is placed in a glass of water. The Little Tooth Mouse drinks the water, collects the tooth, and leaves a coin in the empty glass.

KEEP'EM CLEAN

First graders from Miner Normal School, Washington, D.C. (around 1910

Oral hygiene means keeping your mouth, teeth, and gums clean and healthy. We know now that brushing your teeth is the most important thing you can do yourself. But 100 years ago, toothbrushes and toothpaste were new to lots of people. Teachers helped children develop good tooth brushing habits in school. Many schools around the world still teach oral hygiene.

Dental floss removes plaque that can lead to dental decay. Start by wrapping floss around your middle fingers. Put it between your teeth and move it up and down against them. Do this at least once a day. Floss picks work, too.

TOOTH TRUTH

DON'T WASTE THE PASTE
How much toothpaste is the the right amount to use? You don't need a lot, just a pea-sized squeeze on your brush. Be sure to spit out the toothpaste after brushing—don't swallow it.

Tips for Toothbrushing

Fluoride is a mineral added to toothpaste that helps prevent cavities and keeps your teeth healthy. When you brush your teeth, you apply fluoride to them.

B Brush for two minutes, twice a day.

R Rinse your brush well and let it air dry, bristles facing upward.

U Use a brush with soft bristles. Pick a size that fits comfortably in your mouth.

S Softly brush your tongue—bacteria lurk there too.

H Have a new toothbrush on hand. Change your brush when the bristles get frayed.

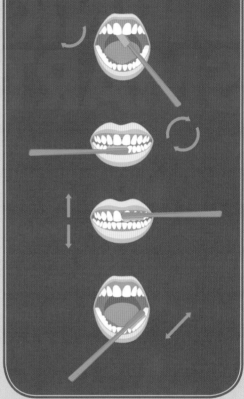

HOW TO BRUSH YOUR TEETH

Brush all surfaces of your teeth—front and back, top and bottom.

KNOW A PRO: DENTAL HYGIENIST

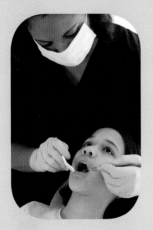

Dental hygienists clean your teeth, ask you questions about them, and show you how to take care of them. They may take X-rays if needed, and apply a fluoride varnish or gel to your teeth to protect your teeth.

EAT SMART, DRINK SMART

What and how you eat makes a big difference to the health of your teeth. Limiting how long and how often foods high in sugars and acids are in your mouth is important. Do this by only having them with meals instead of nibbling or sipping them for hours.

PET PATROL Dogs and other pets need to eat smart, too. Look for special pet treats and dental chews designed to reduce plaque.

STOP

Avoid these gooey foods. They stick to teeth and have a longer time to cause plaque.

Caramels

Hard Candy

Gummies

Dried fruit is sticky. It deposits sugars on your teeth, which feeds the bacteria that causes decay.

Dried apricots

Take Care

Teeth are tough, but they can break. Don't use your teeth to chew ice or hard candy, crack open nuts or seeds, or chew on pencils or fingernails.

If you drink soda, sports beverages, and juices, use a straw. When you use a straw, the liquid spends less time washing over your teeth.

CAUTION

Our bodies need the sugars that occur naturally in dairy, fruits, and vegetables. But citrus fruits, such as oranges and lemons, have acids that can hurt your teeth.

Orange juice

Small amounts of sweets are okay, but problems occur when too much sugar meets up with our teeth.

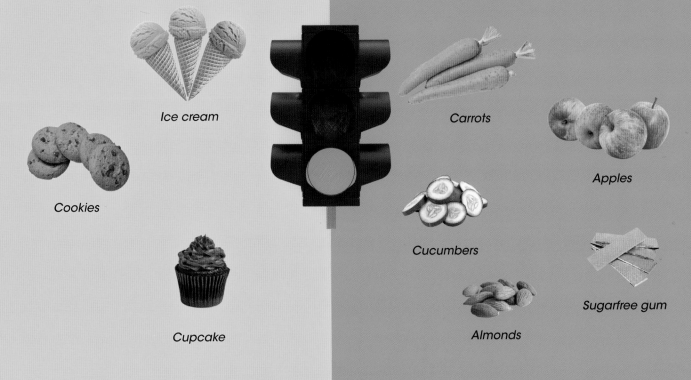

Ice cream

Cookies

Cupcake

GO FOR IT

These foods are good for building strong teeth. They stop acid damage, restore mineral loss in enamel, and coat teeth in a protective film.

Yogurt

Milk

Cheese

Snack on these foods to increase saliva flow. It cleans, repairs, and protects tooth enamel.

Carrots

Apples

Cucumbers

Sugarfree gum

Almonds

PLAQUE ATTACK!

Water, food, and oxygen all travel through your mouth to reach the rest of your body. So the health of your mouth—including teeth, gums, tongue, and jaws—can affect the health of your entire body.

Plaque is the sticky coating that forms on teeth. It holds a mass of bacteria and plaque acids together. Everyone gets plaque on their teeth. It's harmless if removed regularly. If it stays around, it can lead to painful problems.

HOW DOES TOOTH DECAY DEVELOP?

Starchy foods or sugary foods or drinks go into your mouth. They touch the plaque on your teeth and feed the bacteria.

Bacteria in the plaque go wild. Within 20 seconds, they multiply and form harmful plaque acids.

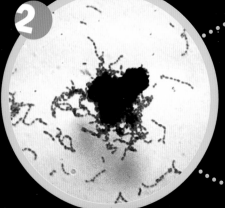

The plaque acids start to dissolve minerals in tooth enamel. New plaque forms. This attack goes on for about 20 minutes.

Plaque

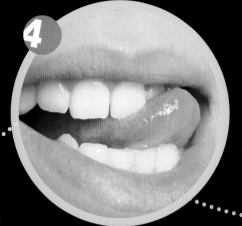

4 Saliva washes over teeth and restores the minerals in the enamel. It plays an important role in preventing and fighting tooth decay. But it can't get to places where there is plaque. This means plaque keeps forming.

5 Over time, plaque acids eat through the tooth enamel and form a hole. This is called a cavity. You may have a toothache.

6 Decay moves on, slowly destroying the tooth structure. Warning signs include bad breath, pain, swollen gums, and spots on teeth.

7 Decay gets worse, infecting the pulp and root of the tooth. If left untreated, the tooth is destroyed.

DANGER

WHAT CAN YOU DO?

✔ Clean your teeth regularly to remove plaque.

✔ Eat more foods that are good for your teeth. Eat fewer foods that are harmful to your teeth.

✔ Have regular dental check-ups. The dental team will clean your teeth and help restore the mineral loss.

✔ If you get a toothache or cavity, see the dentist right away.

WHAT HAPPENS DURING A DENTAL EXAM?

WHEN YOU SEE A DENTIST

A regular visit to the dentist—called a check-up—includes an exam and cleaning. It may also include X-rays and treatment. Hop into the exam chair; your appointment is ready to begin.

First, meet the dental hygienist, who will:

- explain what will happen during the appointment
- look inside of your mouth and make notes for the dentist
- ask you if you have any problems such as pain when you eat or bleeding gums when you brush
- take X-rays of your mouth if the dentist thinks you need them
- clean your teeth

Next, meet the dentist, who will:

- read the hygienist's notes, look at your X-rays, and examine your mouth
- make a diagnosis (identify problems) and discuss them with you

Then:

- There may be treatments to prevent tooth decay. These include having a dental sealant applied to the chewing surfaces of hard-to-clean back teeth to prevent decay from forming. Or a fluoride varnish or gel may be applied to your teeth. (Fluoride is a mineral that helps prevent tooth decay.)
- The hygienist will teach you ways to better care for your teeth. You may get a fluoride mouth rinse or tablets to use at home.
- If repairs are needed, an appointment will be made for another visit.

Cleaning tools are used to remove plaque and tartar.

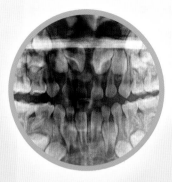

X-rays show how baby teeth are growing in, cavities, and bone changes due to gum disease.

Polishing is done with scrubbing or spraying tools.

KNOW A PRO: DENTIST

A dentist is a medical doctor who works to prevent tooth and gum diseases and to repair oral health problems. Someone who wants to be a dentist has to go to school, study dental sciences, and pass special tests before he or she has a license to say, "Open wide!"

Dental Visits for Dogs and Cats

A pet dental visit may include an oral exam, X-rays, a tooth cleaning, and treatment. Animals may get scared, wriggle around, and even bite during treatment. For their safety and the vet's, they are usually given anesthesia, which causes them to sleep, stay motionless, and not feel pain.

TOOLS
OF THE *TRADE*

From long-handled mirrors to X-ray machines, your dentist has many tools to use to examine your teeth and take care of problems. There are special tools for cleaning teeth and others for doing repairs.

1. Dental Explorer
This is a tool used to examine teeth and look for problems with the enamel. It has a fine point that can detect soft spots, a sign of early decay.

2. Dental Scaler
A dental hygienist uses a variety of hand tools to clean teeth. This scaler scrapes plaque off teeth.

3. Mouth Mirror
This small mirror has a long handle. It is used to examine the back side of your teeth.

4. 3-D Printer

Digital scanning and 3-dimensional printing technology are used to create everything from mouthguards to artificial teeth. Items can be made quickly to fit a particular patient.

5. Panoramic X-Ray Machine

This machine moves in a semicircle around your head while you stand still. It takes a picture of your entire mouth and jaws.

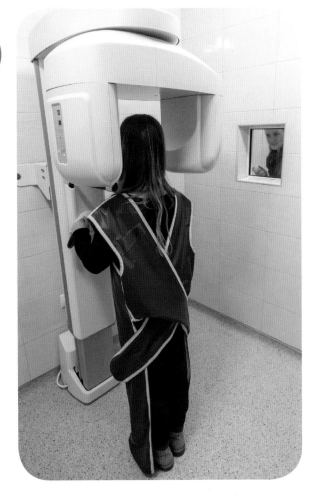

6. Dental Drill

When decay needs to be removed before a tooth cavity is filled, a drill does the job. Special numbing medicine can be given to prevent pain during the process.

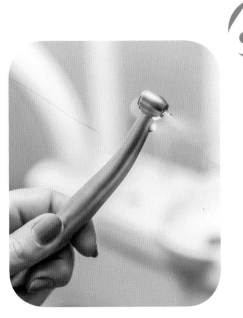

BRACE
FOR IT

Permanent teeth sometimes grow in crooked, crowded together, or too far apart. Or your upper and lower jaws don't always fit together when you bite down. These things can cause problems with eating and speaking. At your dental checkups, the dentist looks at how your new teeth are growing. If there is a problem, the dentist may send you to see an orthodontist.

Fashion Forward

An orthodontist uses different tools and procedures. These include braces and retainers to help straighten teeth. Braces include brackets affixed to  each tooth on the top or bottom row and a wire that connects them all. Springs or rubber bands may also be used. These put pressure on the teeth over a long period of time. It may take as much as two years or so for teeth to move into their proper position. Braces are are made of different materials and in a variety of colors.

Keep 'em in Place

After teeth are straightened, a retainer may be needed. Retainers retain (hold) the teeth in their new positions until all the parts of your mouth are adjusted and the teeth stay in place. Retainers come in a variety of colors and designs.

Keep 'em Safe

Mouth guards protect your teeth and mouth during contact sports such as football and ice hockey. Special mouth guards are usually needed if there are braces on your teeth. An orthodontist can help fit one for you.

A Space Age Look

Some people want braces that you can't see. The very first "invisible" braces were invented thanks to the United States space agency, NASA. They invented a strong, lightweight and transparent material for work with radar and missiles. Other inventors then used the material to create invisible brackets for braces.

Braces for Pets If a dog's teeth are so crooked that it is in pain or has difficulty eating, it may need braces to correct the problem.

KNOW A PRO: ORTHODONTIST

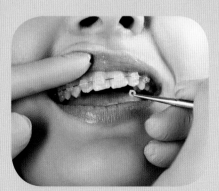

An orthodontist is a doctor who specializes in correcting irregular teeth. After completing dental school, he or she will go through up to three years of special training to become an orthodontist. (*Ortho* means "straight.")

1. Dental Pelican

Named for its resemblance to the long beak of a pelican bird, this tool was used from the 1300s to the 1700s. The claw ends of the metal arms were used to extract (pull out) a decayed tooth. One claw was placed around the bad tooth. The other was placed by the tooth next to it. This provided additional strength, called leverage, to yank out the bad tooth. It most likely also damaged the good tooth.

2. Tooth Key

Popular in the 1700s, this device looked like a door key and turned like one, too. The claw end was placed around a decayed tooth and rotated (turned) by the handle. This loosened the bad tooth. It also often broke the tooth, and damaged the gums and jaw.

3. Chew Stick

Before the bristle-topped toothbrushes we use today were developed, many people used chew sticks—pieces cut from a type of tree called an arak—to clean their teeth. The frayed end was used to clean the teeth. Some cultures still use these chew sticks, called miswaks, today.

KNOW A PRO: BARBER-SURGEON

During the Middle Ages, barbers in Europe did more than cut hair. Beginning around 1,000 years ago, and continuing into the 1700s, barber-surgeons performed surgery, sold medicines, and extracted teeth, too. They learned medicine as apprentices to more experienced practitioners.

TOOTH OR SCARE

4

Before anyone knew what caused toothaches and rotting teeth, some people thought that holes in teeth were caused by tooth worms—imagined creatures that gnawed holes through. But the holes were really cavities. Teeth were cared for, and bad teeth were pulled, using different and sometimes scary-looking instruments.

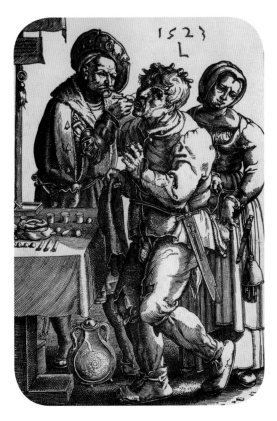

5

4. Tooth picks

How did people long ago remove bits of food from between their teeth? They made picks out of things such as twigs and bird feathers. But those wore down quickly. Porcupine quills were strong and perfectly shaped to do the tough job of cleaning between the teeth.

5. Olden days

Records show that people have been studying and writing about dental care for at least 7,000 years. This picture, showing a surgeon dentist at work, was done nearly 500 years ago.

STORIES
TEETH TELL

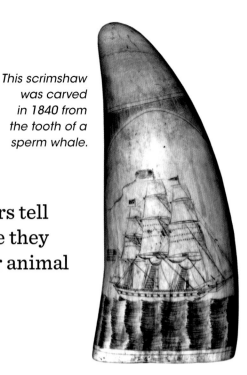

This scrimshaw was carved in 1840 from the tooth of a sperm whale.

Some teeth have stories carved onto them. Others tell the story of a group of people and how and where they live. Teeth can also tell the story of the person or animal that once had them in their mouth.

At a Crow Fair in Montana

A Whale of a Tale

This whale tooth tells a story to anyone looking at it. Called scrimshaw, it was made at a time when large American whaling ships went out to sea. In their spare time, sailors made scrimshaw from whale teeth and bones. They carved a design with a sharp tool, and rubbed stain or ink into the lines. Scrimshaw pieces have carvings on both sides of a tooth that tell stories, often about the ships the sailors were on. Today, hunting whales is not allowed in most of the world.

Family Stories

Ivory elk teeth are prized by many Native American tribes in the western United States. Only the two upper canines are ivory—small, but composed of the same material as elephant tusks. Elk ivories and the family stories that go with them are passed down for generations. They are symbols of good luck, strength, and hard work. The Crow are famous for dresses with up to 300 elk ivories on them. Today, imitation elk teeth made of plastic or bone can be bought to sew on dresses.

Kiowa woman in elk-tooth dress in the 1870s

SCIENCE AT WORK: FORENSIC DENTISTRY

What do teeth have to tell us? Teeth hold many clues about the person or animal that they belong to. A forensic dentist is someone who solves mysteries and crimes by studying teeth, bite marks, and dental records.

• Bite marks of animals and people are as unique as fingerprints. They can tell experts who made them.

• The shapes, sizes, injuries, and repairs recorded in a person's dental records can be used to identify a person by their teeth.

• Traces of radioactive carbon from above-ground nuclear bomb tests in the 1950s and 1960s are in every living thing born since then, including tooth enamel.
It helps forensic scientists determine when a person was born.

• DNA testing is used to solve crimes, identify a body, and even figure out who a person's parents are. Tooth pulp can be used for this. So can a toothbrush.

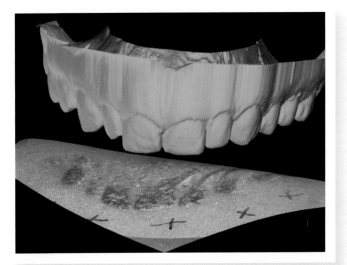

This computer reconstruction shows the use of 3-D imaging technology to match teeth to a bite-mark pattern.

CRIME SCENE DO NOT CROSS

OTHER THINGS WITH TEETH

A sprocket (a type of wheel) has teeth that fit into a chain. When the wheel moves, the teeth move the chain forward. This helps bicycles go.

Gears are a set of wheels with interlocking teeth. They work together to make a machine like this clock go.

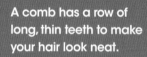

A comb has a row of long, thin teeth to make your hair look neat.

This handheld saw has sharp teeth to cut through wood.

When you pull the tab, the teeth on a zipper link up to hold two pieces of fabric together.

SAY WHAT?

An idiom is an expression that means something different than what it sounds like. For example, if you say something is "a piece of cake," you mean "it's easy." Here are some tooth idioms. See if you can guess what they mean. Then check below for definitions.

1 That test was hard. I passed **by the skin of my teeth.**

2 I want to **sink my teeth into** the cool new art project.

3 Finding out something my sister doesn't want me to know is **like pulling teeth.**

4 He fought **tooth and nail** for the right to have longer recess.

5 When I learned to read, I **cut my teeth on** picture books.

1. barely; 2. to do enthusiastically; 3. extremely difficult; 4. used a lot of effort; 5. started out (like baby teeth growing in)

SPOTLIGHTS ON TEETH

Saint Apollonia

Eastern Orthodox and Roman Catholic churches celebrate the Feast Day of St. Apollonia on February 9th. For more than 1,700 years, people of those faiths have prayed to her to stop their toothaches. Before she died over her religious beliefs, an angry mob attacked her and knocked out her teeth.

The Temple of the Sacred Tooth

About 2,500 years ago, the Buddha died in India. A canine tooth of the Buddha became a holy relic. People believed that whoever had the tooth would rule the land. Battles were fought over the tooth. In 371, Princess Hemamali carried Buddha's tooth from India to Sri Lanka. She hid it in her hair to keep it safe during the journey. The tooth is now kept in a gold box in a magnificent Buddhist temple in Kandy, Sri Lanka. Every summer, there is a 10-day celebration to honor the sacred tooth.

TOOTH TRUTH

George Washington, the first president of the United States, wore false teeth. Contrary to legend, they were not made of wood, which would have turned soft and mushy from saliva. Made by his dentist, John Greenwood, President Washington's false teeth were made from animal teeth, porcelain, lead, and gold.

Space Case

◄ Its official name is RX J0603.3+4214, but scientists call it the "Toothbrush Cluster." Can you guess how this galaxy cluster got its nickname?

Space Face

Astronauts have to find ways to take care of their teeth in space. People and things float on the space station because the gravity force is weak. This makes toothbrushing a challenge. Special lockers keep toothbrushes and toothpaste from floating away.

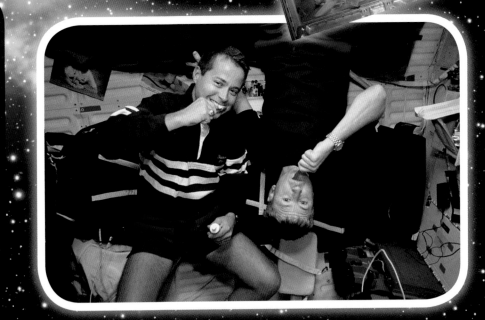

RESOURCES

MUSEUMS

Dr. Samuel D. Harris
National Museum of Dentistry
Baltimore, MD
This museum is home to more than 40,000 objects related to teeth and dentistry. If you visit, you'll find both hands-on exhibits and some hands-off treasures such as George Washington's false teeth. Sneak a peek at some of the treasures by clicking the Exhibitions tab on their website.
dental.umaryland.edu/museum/index.html/

Casa Museo Ratón Pérez
Madrid, Spain
This small museum is dedicated to the magical tooth mouse, El Ratón Pérez. If you don't live near the museum, you can explore the museum's website.
casamuseoratonperez.es

BOOKS

Throw Your Tooth on the Roof: Tooth Traditions from Around the World
Selby Beeler
For more information about about traditions practiced around the world when children lose a tooth, read this book.

What If You Had Animal Teeth?
Sandra Markle
If you're wondering what it would be like to have the teeth of a shark or a narwhal, this book explores animal teeth and their adaptions.

ZOO WEBSITES

Learn about animals, watch them on video cameras, and play games at the San Diego Zoo online: *kids.sandiegozoo.org/*

At the Smithsonian's National Zoo site, meet the animals that live there and watch the giant pandas, elephants, and lions on webcams. *nationalzoo.si.edu/animals*

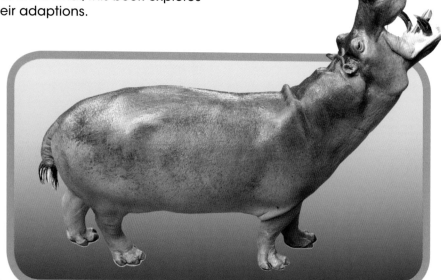

MUSEUM WEBSITES

To see dental tools from long ago and read about a mysterious case in their Tooth Fairy File, check out: *americanhistory.si.edu/blog/2013/02/opening-up-the-tooth-fairy-file-exploring-our-dental-history-collection.html*

If you're interested in brushing *your* teeth in sapce one day, NASA's Kids Club is the place to go for information and interactive fun and games online: *nasa.gov/kidsclub/index.html*

Whaling ships and many other boats from pirates to cargo can be seen at the National Museum of American History's online exhibit, On the Water: *americanhistory.si.edu/onthewater/exhibition/1_1.html*

To learn about dinosaurs and their teeth, explore the more than 300 dinosaur images and facts at the Natural History Museum website: *www.nhm.ac.uk/discover/dino-directory/index.html*

You can go back in time as far as ancient Egypt to learn about the history of medical care when you visit the Science Museum's Brought to Life site: *www.sciencemuseum.org.uk/broughttolife*

See what scientists learned from studying a shark tooth weapon at the Field Museum's website: *https://www.fieldmuseum.org/science/blog/shark-weapons*

Visit the exhibit, Identity by Design, at National Museum of the American Indian's website and learn more elk tooth dress and other dresses. *nmai.si.edu/exhibitions/identity_by_design/IdentityByDesign.html*

Travel to the Temple of the Sacred Tooth to see photos of the temple and celebration held each year to honor the sacred tooth of the Buddha, including the costumed elephants, called Tuskers, that are a part of the pageant, online at: *daladamaligawa.org*

SELECTED SOURCES

Many sources were used in gathering facts about teeth. Here are some of them.

Human Teeth and Health Care: American Dental Association; American Academy of Pediatric Dentistry; American Academy of Pediatrics; National Children's Oral Health Foundation; *The Challenge of Oral Disease – A call for global action, The Oral Health Atlas.* 2nd ed. Geneva: FDI World Dental Federation, 2015; The World Health Organization.
Animal Teeth: Smithsonian National Zoo; University of CA Museum of Paleontology; American Museum of Natural History; San Diego Zoo; Worldwide Milk Production stats from The Food and Agriculture Org. of the United Nations. **Other:** NASA.gov; Carter, Bill, *Ethnodentistry and Dental Folklore.* 1987; Ichord, L. F. (2000). *Toothworms & Spider Juice: An illustrated history of dentistry;* The Field Museum; National Museum of American History. Some additional sources are noted in the Resources above.

ACKNOWLEDGMENTS

From the author:
Thank you to the students and teachers at Mason Elementary School in St. Louis for sharing their families' shed tooth traditions from around the world. Thank you to Barbara Iovaldi for research assistance.

From Scout Books & Media:
We would like to express our gratitude to the talented team at Seagrass Press and Quarto, including Josalyn Moran, Shelley Baugh, and April Balotro-Carothers.

With special thanks to Michael S. Rentz, PhD, Lecturer in Mammalogy at Iowa State University, for his invaluable guidance on animals and their teeth and for boundless enthusiasm in sharing his knowledge with others, and to Jan Killough R.D.H, B.B.A. for contributions on dentistry and procedures, and how best to take care of our teeth.

GLOSSARY

amphibian A vertebrate with smooth skin that can live in and out of water. Frogs and toads are examples of amphibians.

bacteria Microscopic, single-cell living organisms; some can cause disease.

carnivore An animal that eats meat. Tigers and wolves are examples of carnivores.

cavity A hole in a tooth caused by dental decay.

deciduous Something that sheds at the end of its life cycle. Deciduous trees shed their leaves each year. Primary teeth are also called deciduous.

dental decay The damaging effect of bacteria and food on tooth enamel. Over time, dental decay leads to cavities. Tooth brushing, flossing, and certain dental treatments can prevent dental decay.

erupt When a new tooth pushes through the gum and becomes visible. The process is called eruption.

fluoride A mineral, naturally found in water, which can prevent cavities. It is added to toothpaste and fluoride varnishes applied to the surface of teeth to strengthen enamel.

forensics The use of science and technology to solve crimes and mysteries.

fossil The preserved remains or traces of an animal or plant that lived millions of years ago.

herbivore An animal that only eats plants. Rabbits and sheep are examples of herbivores.

hygiene Practices that keep you and things around you clean and healthy.

hygienist A professional who works in a dental office. A hygienist cleans your teeth and teaches you about taking care of them.

invertebrate An animal without a backbone. Worms and butterflies are examples of invertebrates.

ivory The hard, cream-colored material that tusks are made of.

mammal A warm-blooded vertebrate with hair that produces milk for its young. Cows, dogs, and people are examples of mammals.

mandible The lower jawbone of a toothed vertebrate; also, the biting mouthparts of insects and certain other invertebrates.

omnivore An animal that eats plants and animals. Chimpanzees, humans, and raccoons are examples of omnivores.

oral Things related to the mouth.

oral hygiene Practicing good oral hygiene means keeping your teeth, gums, and mouth clean and healthy.

permanent Lasting a long time; another name for your second set of teeth, also called adult teeth.

plaque A sticky deposit of food and bacteria that grows on the surface of teeth and can cause tooth decay.

prey An animal that is hunted and eaten by another animal.

primary First or earliest. Your first set of teeth is called primary.

reptile A cold-blooded vertebrate covered with scales that breathes with its lungs. Snakes and lizards are examples of reptiles.

rodent A gnawing mammal known for sharp, ever-growing incisor teeth. Hamsters and beavers are examples of rodents.

ruminant An animal that has a four-compartment stomach. Ruminants regurgitate food from the rumen compartment and chew it again. Cows, sheep, and goats are examples of ruminants.

saliva The watery liquid in your mouth secreted by glands.

vertebrate An animal with a backbone and internal skeleton. Fish, amphibians, reptiles, birds, and mammals are all vertebrates.

INDEX

Illustrations are indicated by **boldface.** When illustrations fall within a page span, the entire span of pages is **boldface.**

PHOTO CREDITS

1 To scrape out soft clams from their shells.

2 Yes. A common garden snail can have about 14,000 teeth— on its tongue!

 3 No! Using dental floss cleans up to 40% of the surfaces of your teeth.

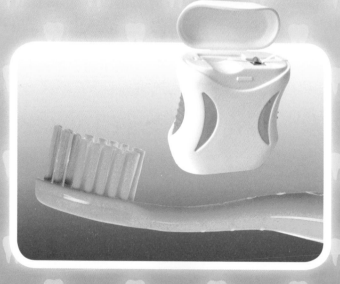